# Barry Sanders

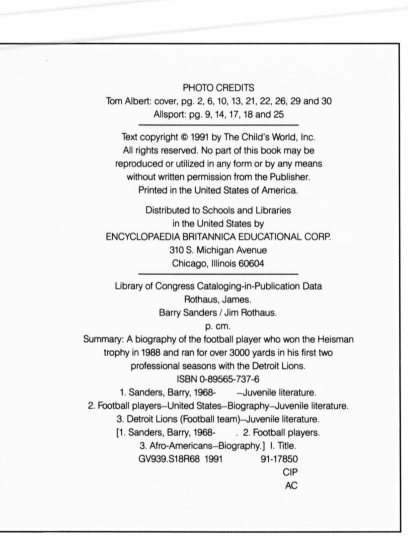

PHOTO CREDITS
Tom Albert: cover, pg. 2, 6, 10, 13, 21, 22, 26, 29 and 30
Allsport: pg. 9, 14, 17, 18 and 25

Distributed to Schools and Libraries
in the United States by
ENCYCLOPAEDIA BRITANNICA EDUCATIONAL CORP.
310 S. Michigan Avenue
Chicago, Illinois 60604

Library of Congress Cataloging-in-Publication Data
Rothaus, James.
Barry Sanders / Jim Rothaus.
p. cm.
Summary: A biography of the football player who won the Heisman
trophy in 1988 and ran for over 3000 yards in his first two
professional seasons with the Detroit Lions.
ISBN 0-89565-737-6
1. Sanders, Barry, 1968-    —Juvenile literature.
2. Football players–United States–Biography–Juvenile literature.
3. Detroit Lions (Football team)–Juvenile literature.
[1. Sanders, Barry, 1968-     . 2. Football players.
3. Afro-Americans–Biography.] I. Title.
GV939.S18R68  1991          91-17850
                                      CIP
                                      AC

# Barry Sanders

*by James R. Rothaus*

Barry is a team player.

**Barry is a team player.**

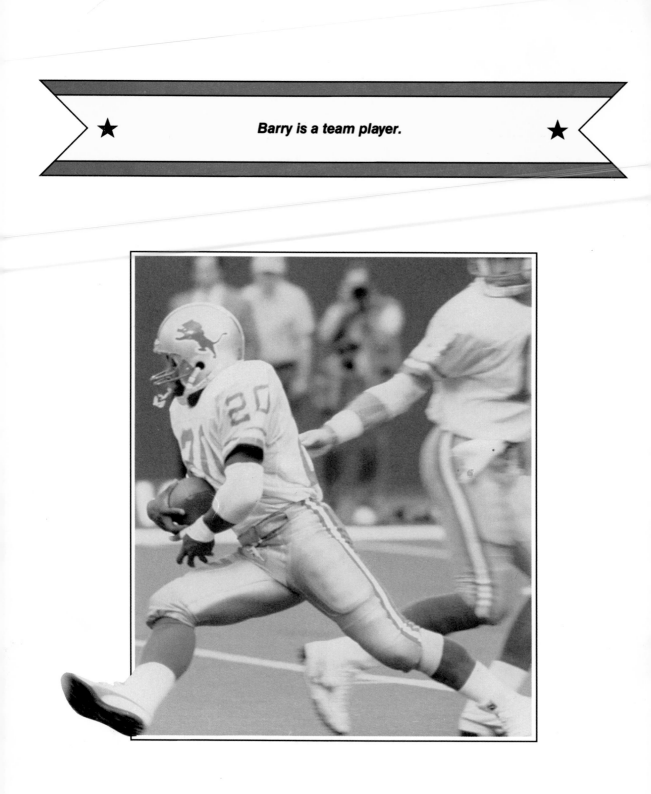

The Detroit Lions were leading the Atlanta Falcons 31-24. There was one minute left in the last game of the 1989 season. The Lions had the ball, so there was almost no chance of an Atlanta comeback. On the sideline Detroit star running back Barry Sanders was sitting on the bench. Sanders, who had rushed for 158 yards, was ready to enjoy another victory. Then one member of the Detroit coaching staff figured out that Sanders needed only ten more yards to win the National Football League rushing title.

Lions head coach Wayne Fontes called Sanders over. "You're ten yards from leading the league in rushing," Fontes said to Sanders. "Do you want to go in?" Sanders just shook his head. "Coach," he said, "let's just win it and go home." Sanders didn't care about winning the NFL rushing title. He cared only about winning the game. "When everyone is out for statistics, that's when trouble starts," Sanders stated after the game. "I don't want to ever do that."

One of Barry's fans is Walter Payton.

**A**year later, Barry Sanders got his NFL rushing title. But the Lions didn't make the play-offs, so he wasn't that happy about the 1990 season. His teammates, though, were very happy Sanders was a Lion. He had been a pro player for only two years, but Sanders had rushed for almost 3,000 yards. Many experts were calling him the best runner in the game today. Some even thought Sanders might be the best ever. One of Barry's biggest fans is Walter Payton, the NFL's all-time leading rusher.

Payton saw Sanders play twice in 1989. "I don't know if I was ever <u>that</u> good," Payton said after watching Sanders gain 120 yards against the Chicago Bears. Like Payton, Sanders is a powerful runner. But Sanders is quicker than Payton was. "I remember waiting to hit him [Sanders]," recalled Trace Armstrong, a defensive end for Chicago. "He just stopped and turned, and he was gone. He's like a little sports car."

14

**S**anders might be flashy on the field, but he is a very quiet guy on and off the field. Sanders really doesn't like to talk about himself. It's almost as if he would rather not be a star. Maybe that's because Barry Sanders isn't used to being well known. Sanders was a good player in high school, but the college scouts weren't that impressed. "We didn't even look at him," says Woody Widenhofer, former coach at the University of Missouri. "I don't think too many schools did."

When Sanders graduated from North High in Wichita, Kansas, only two colleges wanted him to play for them. Sanders picked Oklahoma State over Wichita State. Two years later the guy hardly anybody wanted led the nation's major colleges in kickoff return yards. But Barry Sanders wasn't a starting running back at Oklahoma State until his junior year. Sanders had to wait until Thurman Thomas graduated to make first string.

T homas went off to play pro ball for the Buffalo Bills. Sanders then became the starting tailback for Oklahoma State when the 1988 season began. When the year ended, Barry Sanders' name was in the NCAA record books. He ran for 2,628 yards and thirty-nine touchdowns in 1988. Both were NCAA records. "He just takes your breath away when he runs," said Oklahoma State coach Pat Jones. By this time the whole country knew who Barry Sanders was.

**S**anders was the favorite to win the 1988 Heisman Trophy, which is given to the top college player every year. The day the Heisman was to be given out, Sanders was in Japan, where Oklahoma State was playing Texas Tech. The award was to be given hours before the Oklahoma State-Texas Tech game. The Downtown Athletic Club, which gives out the Heisman, wanted Sanders to be in a Japanese television studio when the award was presented.

22

Sanders was to be part of a live hookup with the Heisman award show in New York. Why? The reason was simple. Everybody expected little Barry Sanders to win the Heisman. Sanders, however, didn't want to go to the studio. He wanted to study instead. But Oklahoma State officials talked Sanders into going on television. When the Heisman winner was named, Sanders cracked a small smile. The winner's name was Barry Sanders.

**S**anders was only a junior during the 1988 season. He had another year left at the college level. But Barry Sanders had nothing left to prove in college football. After talking with his parents, he decided to turn pro. Detroit took Sanders with the third pick in the 1989 NFL draft. The Lions really needed a great running back. Sanders was their man. They agreed to pay him $6.1 million over five years. That included a $2.1 million bonus for signing his contract.

**S**anders then wrote a
check for $210,000 and gave it to
his church. Religion had always been
important to Barry. He wanted to
give something back to his church.
Meanwhile, Detroit fans wondered
when Sanders would start paying
off for the Lions. They didn't have
long to wait. In his first game with
Detroit, Sanders didn't play until
the second half. But he gained
seventy-one yards in less than half
a game. As the 1989 season went
along, Sanders carried the ball more
and more.

**S**anders shocked Detroit players, coaches, and fans with his running ability. He had a lot of long runs, but some of his shorter gains were the most amazing. "For me," says former Detroit offensive coach Mouse Davis, "his best run was against the [Chicago] Bears. He took the handoff, and the Bears were all over him. He spun, went down into a squat, spun again, made a guy miss him, and ran for a two-yard loss. Absolutely amazing."

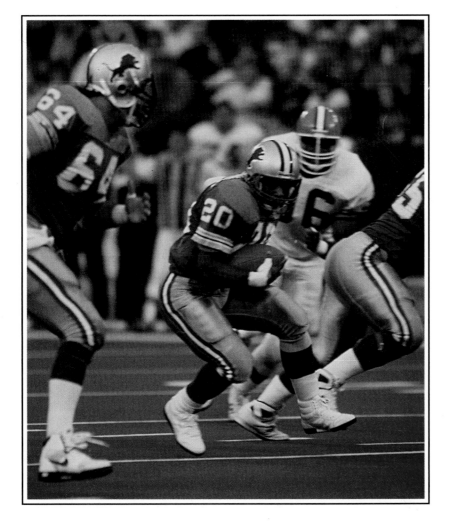

30

"**Y**ou can't begin to pick out one favorite run," says Detroit head coach Wayne Fontes of Sanders. "Why? Because he's had some three-yard runs that may have been the greatest three-yard runs in the history of the game. Those were even more exciting than his twenty-yarders." But Sanders still makes a lot of twenty-yard runs. He is perhaps the most exciting running back in the game today. He might even be the most exciting ever. But Barry Sanders doesn't care about that. All he wants to do is win.